DUALITY

By

La Rae

Order this book online at www.trafford.com
or email orders@trafford.com

Most Trafford titles are also available at major online book retailers.

Print information available on the last page.

ISBN: 978-1-4907-6854-0 (sc)
ISBN: 978-1-4907-6856-4 (hc)
ISBN: 978-1-4907-6855-7 (e)

Library of Congress Control Number: 2015921385

Trafford rev. 06/17/2016

 www.trafford.com

North America & international
toll-free: 1 888 232 4444 (USA & Canada)
fax: 812 355 4082

TO

MARY NORDSTROM

An Earth Angel

SPECIAL THANKS TO

Kelley Foy and the gang at Crema for
keeping me hydrated and fed while I wrote

Marlen Espinola for keeping
me sane and beautiful

The Kevins (Clark & Eich) and
Maryann Bonfig for making me laugh
when I become too serious at work

Leighanne Morton one of the most intelligent,
funny and caring persons I know

Enzo my most recent grandson who now
graces the Earth with his presence

Rachel the beautiful butterfly
mother of my grandchildren

Doctors Johnny Mei, Correa and Alberti
for encouragement and support for my
artwork and writing. All this accomplished
after my full-time job as a nurse

Dr. Singer for you valuable support and
your constant questioning when this
book would be finished THANK YOU

Once again to all those seen and unseen
who have encouraged and helped me along
the way -smiles and hugs to all of you

Amazing thanks and gratitude to the Earth for
letting me abide on this beauty-filled home

DUALITY

Duality creates choice
Time allows for correction
Earth is the playpen

The poems in this book are reflections of many years accumulation as I am experiencing self-awareness in duality

Peace
La Rae

FISH

What would you wish
If a multihued interdimensional fish
Swam into view
And asked you
What would you renew
And what you would disperse
If your wishes
Were tenderly supported
And truly came into
Your soul's eye-view

LIFE MOVES ON

Life moves on
Past runs around
In circles

Present is unclear
As to what is seen
In a life filled with
Murky agitated water
Stirred by scenes
With no means to clear itself very soon

Past will cry
Present will die
Future will sigh
'What happened'

FORGOTTEN

You have forgotten
We live on a planet begotten
Many evolutions ago

You continue to try and forget
Inherent sets
Placed into your DNA

No manipulations are required
Just your uplifted desires
To help this planets change
Into another way of being

Duality's close
Is ridding the time worn clothes
That humanity once thought
Covered their energy

For I am Gravity's release

YOUR LOVE

I saw you
Taking gentle care
Of the one you love
Even tho
His awareness
Dove-tailed into oblivion

He could only greet you
With the demons contained
In his cloud covered soul

Your sorrow filmed eyes
Contained wise knowing
But your fractured and broken heart
Was showing thru

ENERGY PIRATES

Dreams die
Pigs fly
Enlightened forces lament
Others give consent
To energy's raping

Most humans continue scraping
To get by

Meanwhile in the sky
Pirates of galaxies past
Raid stores of human energy's vast
Creative loops in time

SET UP

This is a set up
Please do not get up
And start introducing
Your smile ridden diseases

Can you not know
Your energy's glow
Tells of death
As you spew forth
What pleases you only

Who am I
Earth's Integrity

CULTIVATION

How do you know
What photos will show
In the future

What we think is ideal/perfect now
Is like a plow
Cultivating Time and Space
For futures growth to behold
Of humanitys presence in the present
Wherever they might be located

Who knows
What coming generations will sow
After they reap
What we
In Presents moment
Have put in
Their brains creative hands
For supposedly
Safe keeping

OLD FASHIONED SHOES

Thoughts of you
Worn like old fashioned shoes
Beloved and resoled many times over

Shoes that have traversed
Green clover filled lands
Almost blue-hued waving grass strands
Experienced in interwoven dimensional
Meadows of duality

Flowers
Like tendrils of a lovers caress
Touch all areas in a quest
Of those well worn beloved soles

What cares are left to traverse
What areas will be walked in reverse
And changed into something new

All because of love
For those oft resoled shoes
And the human steps
They take
And the imprints they make

TREASURE CHEST

What makes one blush
With glances first questioning touch

What makes ones heart feel
And want to reveal
What the treasure chest
Of I AM
Retains and remains
Out of view from another's
Love fueled gaze

What deeper hues and shades
Traces and claims of colors
That treasure chest contains
Encircling the rich-filled contents
Labeled the true you

What would you lay bare
What would you desire to share
With the 'you'
Of another being

Would you be afraid
What secrets would you delightfully trade
When you terminally discard
Your deepest fears

Will you tempt
Anothers eyes ears and heart
With the truth of your being

OR

Will you close down
Not uttering a single sound
Which could have caused
Another's passing gaze to turn around
And reveal and share
Their treasure chest
With YOU

SLAMMED WORDS

We will see
What tonight's visions will be
While I listen to poetry
Slammed into time-fueled ears

Will words rhyme
Will they be intensely timed
With vocal notes spoken high/low
Fast/slow

What visions divine
Will be contained in my mind
From those machine gun
Fired words

It may sound absurd
But I feel a little intimidated
Already

TIME

Does it fly
Does it seem to stand still
What is its meaning
Do we honor it
Do we rail against it

One thing is certain
Time flows on unchecked
How long will we measure it
On scales of direction & involvement
On this beloved land in space

THE FALL

Air is thinning
Arcs of healing
Are beginning
Their waves of electromagnetic change

Humans are changing
Their ways of relating
Contemplating and entertaining
New ways of being
Sent forth by the decree of
All That Is

Brains are resolving and dissolving
Problems that were started
When tricksters implanted
Fear based tunes
In neurons
Embedded in heretofore beings of Peace's Grace

The fall of humans
Was amazing
Their energy was supposedly
downgraded and degraded

But The One is aware
And knows all
Decreed that the so called fall
Was a lesson for both
Perpetrators and recipients

We have choice
We have knowledge
Wisdom is exploding
All around the Earth

Perceive your truth
For you are much more
Than what has been
Implanted and force fed you

FREQUENCIES

Do frequencies think
Do they blink
Do they sink into oblivion
Or
Do they survive
Do they thrive
Do they ply their trade

What fields do they relate to
Do they relate at all

Do they conspire
To bring all higher
To reach The One

SPONTANEOUS COMBUSTION

You stop and stare
As if I were not totally aware
Of you and what you can do
Plus your energy's core

What is your insistence
In this current existence
To keep stoking the fire in your eyes
For me

Have we not met before
And opened a door
To spontaneous combustion
Of whom we are - simultaneously

'I'll miss you' you say
But what price will I pay
If we joined energy fields

Duality's timed space
Does not equate to us as one

LIMITED PERCEPTIONS

You can cease
Your stares
Your limited perceptions
Your absurd cravings
For an enlightenment
That not one iota of your being
Can accept understand or contain
Within Duality's limited framework

Change your gazes view
To what resides in you
And what you want to remain and retain
When Duality's embrace
Ceases to exist

GRIEF BEGONE

Grief begone
Your heart breaking song
Is coming to an end
It was never humanity's friend
To begin with

It ended up being a symphony
Instead of a short tune
Humans were supposed to learn from
It's taken so long
For Grief's thoughtforms
To begin to come undone

Wear a smile so big
As happiness grows
In its unfoldment
For an incoming enlightened race
Is arriving on this precious place
Nevermore to degrade
An uplifted field

I HEAR

I hear
What you once held dear
You have pushed far away

I hear
What once was so clear
Has been muddied and destroyed

I hear
Things you once held true
Are now covered in emotional blue

I hear
What was so close to your heart
Has been destroyed by a poisoned dart
Of betrayal

I hear
Those whom you loved
Have been hit by a nail studded glove
Of disgrace

I hear
What was once gentle and sweet
Has been beaten Into the pulp
Of nothingness

I hear
That your leaving
Has left others seething
In pain

Are you now satisfied

SATURDAY

Here I am
Alone again
On a Saturday night
The TV is on
My phone is numb
So am I

The loneliness is vast
My feelings frozen
In the ice age of time
Will they ever thaw and flow again

Does the broken heart eventually sing

OR

Does it sing its lonely song to emptiness

He who controls your thoughtforms
Controls you
(Laraeism)

ELEGANT HARM

I gave you my heart
You gave me words

I gave you my heart
You just played a dirge

I gave you a special moment in time
You just looked at me as tho I had committed a
crime

I gave you my heart
You started to whine

I gave you my heart
You caused me alarm

I gave you my heart
You caused me elegant harm

For I am Earth's heart

PASSION

Is passion a bold distraction
Of Creativity's current energy

Will some be amused
Will some try to abuse
The tools that prove
Future's reality is present

FEELING

I feel too deeply
Or
Is it not enough

It is a thick varnish
Will it crack
And I be released
Or

Will it stay and wear me down
Til I am glossy and hard too

I don't know so
I wait the weight

INTELLECT'S DECEPTION

I learned another valuable lesson today
Intellect's deception thought it was divine

Yes I remember words spoken
From a previous one
Who thought he was sublime

'Make them pay dearly for your words'
He said in such a casual way
The true meaning held vocal sway

Well you've had your day
In science
In control
In money
In power

But a change is on the way
I learned a valuable lesson
And God's Grace will win the day

BUYERS BE AWARE

This is a drama
A real true life story
This is not a tale of fame and glory
But an agreement made in
This loop of rhyme
To be experienced
In these changing times

Of questioning
What is really mine
In thought
In word
In speed of enfoldment
To rare to be a chance happening

WARNING

Energy
Save
Slave
Behave
To the grave and back again

Sin
Spin grin
Wherein
Humans die
For pigs that fly
On beams unseen by human eyes

Regress
Detest
Digest
False information intravenously fed
As humans are bled
Of creative energy integrity

Rehearse
Diverse
Games of destruction
'Please come to the induction'
Of a master plan
Long since dead

EARTHS NEW GRAVITATIONAL FIELD

How do you know
What will be allowed and encouraged to grow
In Earth's new gravitational field

What flowers and/or weeds
Will be released
To roam free
And partake of the great experiment
Labeled humanity in Duality

What will humanity choose to feed on
Or release
When this new feast
Is served upon humankinds freshly washed plates
In this time fueled place
Called Earth

Will duality
Be resurrected
Or will massive changes
End the face of Duality's embrace

RELEASE

You twist and turn your eyes and ears
So you can try to exude
Your own fears
Out into the energy around my being
You are prevented from seeing me
As I truly am

What sense of release
Would finally bring Peace
To your body's withering soul

I have no prose
That will heal you
Because my name is war

YOU SAY - Sad Song

You say 'you don't know me'
Well that just may be true
But to whom does it matter more to
Me or you

You say 'what do you want'
I reply 'what do you mean'
You say 'oh just forget it'
Things are much more serious
Than they seem

You say 'you're not my kind'
I say 'how do you know'
You never looked into my heart
Nor peered into my soul

You say 'you're past your prime'
And tho those words hurt me so
Since when is aging considered a crime

You say 'I love you but I cannot live with you'
Now just between us two
By that statement you just made
Who sounds like the biggest fool

You say 'you are no longer the one'
And tho those words stung so
I remember not so long ago
You were singing a different song

You say 'I don't love you anymore'
I will accept those words as true
At least I will finally be freed
From loving the likes of you

You say 'let's make love one more time'
I say 'this proves you are so cruel'
For I do not desire to be involved
In your morality duel

You say 'I'm walking out the door'
Scraping your well heeled boots on the floor
I paste a smile on my face
Knowing I'll see you no more

I say 'I gave you love'
I say 'I gave you support'
And now I know for all those years
I have nothing left to show
But tears and a broken heart

LIFE

Life is a perpendicular line
Through timed - space
Wherein I have driven a stake
And wait

For fate
To begin

Thinking
The curse of intelligent people
(Laraeism)

YOUR MISSHAPEN I

You have again survived
The misshapen I
Of your existence

You were once true
To the form labeled You
Until abuses voice
Whispered its seductive death-filled song in your ear

The familiar refrain
Caused you to turn
And retrace fated steps
To Abuses place
You once mistook for safe
Before you could accept true Love's grace
You flew from its tender and compassionate face

Now take a bow
You have recreated a fatal flaw
And a backwards flow
Where your human energy will rest forevermore

We each choose our path
Thru choices made in view of Duality's face
Of existence
Which you have pulled your shroud over

You were given much
A magical gifted touch
Which will not remain
Because of the choice you
Once again
Have made

Experiences and lessons learned in Duality
Are nothing to ignore

COFFEE AND WAR

Coffee helps the world wake up
And run on grounds
Just as those who love this planet and plane of
existence
Are fueled on words of cooperation and love

There are those
However
Who have hearts and souls of deceivers
Of the highest degree

Can't you see
Not everyone wants or desires
Humans or even the Earth
To be or to survive

These evil ones have decreed
War on life
AND
This planet

INSTANTANEOUS CREATION

Oh what a sensation
Instantaneous creation
Would unfold in Earths atmosphere

Do you think humanity is wise enough
To experience this high quality of evolvement
At this moment in Duality's time

Can you perceive
What instantaneous creation
Would expose and compose
As Clarity would ultimately prevail

So before you continue travail here
Make sure your brains intent is clear
Of lower imaginings
Because highly evolved beings
Know what instantaneous creation entails
And are watching you
Knowing your core energies will be exposed

Human beings will
In Futures time
Be composed
Of simple intricacies
Beyond your current comprehension
For I am Futures tale

FOCUS

Keep your focus here
Awareness is near
Words are to be reached
Reeled in and cradled
With tender fingers

Then tossed into the air
Received by those who care
And desire to share
Their memory fueled moments

Before being crushed
By the gravity of closed minds

SHINE ON

Shine on
Young ones of the future
What magnificent stories
Await to unfold and be told

Dismiss the fears of times gone by
For they no longer apply
To Earths future
Or yours

Be bold
As you unfold your goals
With Peaces kind and gentle embrace
For this precious Earth
And the You Are
Super magnetized futures

Thoughts cause energy to move
I am thought of
(Laraeism)

WAITING

Here I am
Currently waiting
And anticipating
What my hairs future holds

If I may be so bold
I don't know
How color and parameters
Of cut and shape
As I now relate
May cause you to instigate
A change
In my currently held
Belief
Regarding my hairs imminent future

ANOTHER BOOK FINISHED

Here I sit
And contemplate IT
My next completed book

No one realizes the years it took
Of poetry
Of feelings
Of experiences in Duality
And the reflections
That have stirred my soul
And excavated my emotions

Maybe none will comprehend
My devotion
To this planet
And those who exist upon it

The complexities
Of rhythms and rhymes
The subtle intricacies of time
What it be holds and unfolds
In this experience and experiment
Of Duality
Ah humans you have been so blessed

Education produces knowledge
Wisdom produces clarity
They do not equal each other
(Laraeism)

Printed in the United States
By Bookmasters